Suffering

In

Christ

(2018)

*

essay

*

Traumear

Christ as our greater self – that, specifically, is what this little essay wishes to introduce, to those whose ambitions run in that direction. That we suffer our pain rather than reacting to it and to its apparent causes, this is important, but that we suffer it in Christ, this is what delivers us into our final satisfaction and rest.

*

Suffering in Christ

Most everyone knows about pain. It hurts. It is unpleasant. Very few look forward to it. Those who like to cause pain for others we do not consider in this essay; only those who hurt, who are in pain, who are afflicted, grieved, downcast or depressed. Any kind of trial, discomfort and anxiety fits into our category of pain. We might sum up by considering pain of body, mind, spirit, soul and flesh.

The more reflectively we are aware of ourselves, the more are we able to know what part of us is hurting. Is it a headache, a heartache or a sore knee, that sort of thing. Are we having difficulty identifying our soul or does our human spirit seem to be playing us false. What kind of disappointment is it? Are we not getting what we want or are we disgusted with what we did get. Is it a nagging doubt that won't let us get any peace or can we not forgive and forget some imagined slight to our ego. On and on.

Should we mention pain due to illness, sickness and disease? No, best not to enter upon the topic of causes, imagined or otherwise, at this stage. Why not? Because much of our pain stays with us once we have decided what is causing it and we concentrate on that cause, perhaps to remove it or merely to indulge in blaming, accusing and cursing – which makes matters worse. When I ran a lengthy sliver of wood into my hand not that long ago while sanding the edge of a piece of cheap plywood, I right away knew it had to come out as quickly as possible and headed for the surgery. During that time my hand

1

hurt so much that I nearly drove into a pedestrian. I had forgotten to suffer the pain and as a consequence I was agitated and careless. These days I get cramps quite often. No one can tell me what causes them but when I suffer them in Christ they go away. I also banged my shin against the trailer hitch last week and the pain brought tears to my eyes. It was 'exquisite' pain – and ten minutes later all that was left was an extremely sensitive area on my shin which only hurt when I touched it.

I mention the sliver, the cramps and the contusion as three examples of pain related to cause of pain. For the time being I would prefer to ignore cause of pain and concentrate exclusively on pain we may decide to suffer – which does not prevent us, by the way, from having an eye out for what the cause of it may be.

What I find much more interesting at this point is the reason for pain. I do, at this stage of my life, have a few carefully worked out notions of what I mean by 'the reason for pain' and I will have to mention one or two of them, because they are good reasons and if we understand them we are going to take more kindly to the business of 'suffering pain'.

After all it makes a great difference to how we deal with something, especially with something unpleasant, whether we consider we are being treated unfairly and unjustly, so that we resent the consequences, or else we understand that something has occurred to our advantage and we do well to make our peace with it. When we are ever so full of ourselves we automatically strike back with a vengeance and while we are drifting indifferently we are liable to howl and to keep on drifting.

So for our present inquiry I would like to assume that we are, at this moment and hopefully for some time to come, fairly at ease in ourselves, not overly bothered about the future and comfortable with our memory of the past. This is not much to ask but we need at least that if we are to be able to take in what is coming our way in the spirit of learning and enlightenment.

*

The reason for pain:

In a nutshell, human beings are on earth for a good reason and if they forget they are reminded. The reminder usually hurts.

We try to bring up our children in a way that will continue to remind them that they are around for a good reason and in a similar way we adults remind one another. I call it a *sense of nobility* which we nourish in our human community, an attitude that is based on our belief that we, as humans, are responsible for our earth-environment. This belief – this assumption, let's call it – springs from our very being. When we remind one another of it, we do not say: Believe this or we will shun you, but rather: Believe this and you will be more human. We can, after all, be less or more human, and our contentment depends on the more.

So in general we exist for good reason and this reason can be identified and talked about in a great variety of ways, all of which will mean human responsibility for earth-environment. The opposite is egotistic advantage-seeking for self, which leads to extinction and this may not even be painful. Is it not therefore almost as if it were a test for us, that we know ourselves to be, by definition and birth, noble creatures, endowed with various gifts that allow us – and encourage us – to behave in a way that furthers the wellbeing of all creatures, including human beings, on earth? And are we not therefore glad whenever we are reminded that we have accidentally strayed off our true path?

In the particular now, we human beings soon find out, as we grow up, that we cannot, in the end, depend on anyone else to tell us what to do and how to behave, because our definition resides within us. You can teach me why human beings in general, me included, are on earth but my own way of being around, actively and passionately, has to be discovered by me. I have to find my own particular way of adding to the advantage of beings around me.

Now the general and the particular, of course, as always, go hand in hand. What counts is that we give up any notion that anyone else can tell us exactly what is important and good for us to do, this on one side, and on the other side that we remain open to be informed and guided by conditions and circumstances. A good teacher will draw our attention to the true teacher within us. A true guide will persuade us to pay attention to how we are stimulated by things around us and to how we tend to react and intend to respond to the various situations in which we find ourselves.

Pain plays a role in all of this. It relates to our own particular way of being and to our general attitude to what goes on around us. While we are ignorant, pain hurts. We suppose that it hurts us to feel pain. To the extent of our enlightenment, pain is revealed as a series of signposts that would point us in the right direction and urge us along the true path. And the fact that we initially react to pain, as to an enemy, lets us know that pain affects us for a good reason and that we need to be just that little bit more alert in order to read the sign correctly. Thoughtlessly, indifferent to our true advantage, we stray along some convenient and wrong path. Will we ever take kindly to being reminded of our mistake? Rarely. Let's face it, we need to be prodded and we are, after all, glad of it. We know ourselves. Or at least, as we grow up, we do well to get to know ourselves, to become alert to our laziness, our careerist indifference to others, our morbidity and our sensuality, on and on; our negatives are as various and intense as our positives and happily we are not allowed to rest for very long in the misconception of ourselves as good.

*

The suggestion that pain may hurt or not hurt, in other words that we may taste death or not taste it, is not modern-conventional. We do feel a difference, of intensity perhaps, between 'I am in pain' and 'my head hurts'. That pain hurts or does not hurt, this is like saying, on one hand: I am disturbed by this pain, it aggravates me, causes me unease, and on the other hand: I am aware of this pain as I am aware of any other appearance of my environment, physical or otherwise and I may take occasion to deal with it, to utilize it as a suggestion, or to defer. More explicitly now, while the pain hurts, I am reacting to the suggestion that I would be wise to behave in accordance with it. I do understand that pain, in general,

5

implies that either a remedy or an advantage is on the cards for me. This I have learned, in one way or another, and I believe it. I accept it and wish to act in accordance with what I understand and believe to be true, as usual.

Nonetheless I find that initially I am annoyed with every pain. It disturbs me, it shocks me – in short it draws my attention as if saying: 'Look here, something important! Drop everything else and pay heed.' It does this with a degree of intensity. If I am too busy and able to continue with my business, the reminder will probably return in a while. It may eventually insist on itself.

It is a pain that hurts and does so for the reason that we should pay attention and behave in accordance. Our behaviour, as soon as we get down to it, will be more or less appropriate. It will be completely appropriate once the pain no longer hurts.

So what could we possibly mean by pain that no longer hurts? Have we simply managed to put up with it? Do we grit our teeth and say to ourselves: Well, life is painful?

A lot depends here on how long we have made a habit of reacting to pain. I mean not automatically reacting to it, the way we flinch, recoil, shrink into ourselves but rather making a point, and eventually a habit, of withdrawing, consciously, from that which hurts, thereby becoming, to that extent, self-centred.

I realize that I am describing what may, by this present stage of our existence, have turned into a negative and generally ignorant attitude to death and to our incipient mortality. While we are not aware of our true mortality, not much at all of what I am saying here will make sense, so a few words about mortality might be to the point.

We are mortal, we human beings, in that we are liable to die if we are not careful. We are not mortal in the sense that we are bound to die, eventually. That is the popular notion of it, so we have to decide which way we want to go: popular or human. The popular death is eventual and unavoidable non-existence and after that either nothing or some supposed re-emergence in some supernatural realm which allows itself to be pictured in a variety of pleasant and flattering, or unpleasant and cautionary ways. The human death, by comparison, makes sense only in relation to human immortality and to human freedom. As we develop and eventually evolve, we need to be free to choose our own specific means, methods and manoeuvres, because after all we are uniquely individual persons with characteristic contributions to make to our earth-community. We need to be free even to make our own mistakes – from which we learn. As human beings we know we are around on the earth for a good reason and purpose, so there is absolutely no need for us to die if we learn and perform faithfully and intelligently. If we do die, we learn from this too and live again. Human life, in other words, is eternal and death is a mere hiccup. When we depart from the earth we return in spirit in our works. We can imagine this in various ways if we like but any attempt to picture it is counterproductive. If we tried to picture it, we would learn to our benefit that we can in fact imagine it quite usefully.

So the human death may occur several times while we are on earth and it need never occur. When, for example, we lay down our life for others, we do not die; that would not be the way to describe it. We may do that in the light of our immortality, which is to say that the life we have is eternal. We can say that we are both mortal and immortal but it would help to add that our immortality presupposes and is predetermined by our mortality. So much for that.

*

Back now to our discussion of pain that hurts and pain that does not hurt.

Initially we tend to react to pain and this is what hurts. Now in the light of our understanding of this, we may assume the responsibility for the fact that pain hurts, when it does hurt. And this is crucial. It has to be looked at carefully. A great deal hinges on what we mean by responsibility. In an important sense it means that we realize that if we had been different we would not have reacted and the pain would merely have accounted to discomfort. No reaction is involved during a discomfort.

So the accent is on having 'been' different, not on having done different. This is bound to remind many of us of that familiar philosophical difference between being and doing, which plays into the realm of philosophy, of morality and ethics. In the popular vein there is no overlap of being and doing. However we know that a human being is responsible – and accepts the responsibility – not only for what he does but also for how he is. For example, when someone asks you: How are you doing this? You may understand that in the sense of : How are you while you are doing this? And not just as: What is your method? For some, being is most definitely also a doing, and they would be most surprised if we were to hold them at all less than responsible for how they are.

All of us however, when we notice that once again we have reacted to pain and that something hurts, are smart to think and feel something like: Oh, I'm sorry about that; now let me accept this hurt as something for which no one and nothing is to blame, so that I may advance towards the intelligent suffering of the pain.

*

Soul-pain is surely the most difficult to deal with because we react emotionally, passionately, temperamentally and at times forcefully. Several modern centuries of culture and civilization have dealt most charitably and tolerantly with all these affectations. Some moral systems make virtues out of them. The reason for this is that we compare an emotional person to someone who is not capable of emotion, or a passionate person to someone who is not capable of passion, and so on. In other words we set an afflicted individual beside a dead one and no wonder who comes out on top. Surely those who do not live but insist on going through life, incapable of being moved, cannot interest us. To those who are at least alive, to them our hearts go out, as we hope that theirs will go out to us when we are afflicted by our reactionary behaviour, perhaps to the point where we need a reminder from outside before we catch ourselves on. Woefully we notice that once again we have missed the point and have indulged in criticism, in accusation and blame. We judge so as not to be judged. We contemplate vengeance.

At the same time we may let it occur to us that at least we are alive and human. We do not envy the one who boasts that nothing and no one can hurt him, mostly because we fear he may be right and in that case we would wish to keep our distance.

*

So the path from the affliction and the affectation to the intelligent suffering of the pain is worthy of careful consideration. And the sooner we set out on this path each time the better. We can deal with discomfort but when we hurt we are in danger of losing the plot.

Or let us rather say that the intelligent suffering begins with the way we deal with the aftermath of our reaction, that would make more sense. Then we would incline to think of suffering as embracing the two parts, namely accepting responsibility for the reaction and its aftermath and also for dealing with the pain that does not hurt or no longer hurts, which we called discomfort. Such discomforts can be grim, let's face it. If we have ever experienced the total absence of comfort we will no longer say that something is *merely* uncomfortable.

Let us for a moment look at comfort. Of course we can make ourselves comfortable, there is some meaning to that, but mostly comfort has to come to us. Someone who knows how to comfort us and chooses to do so when we need comfort is a valued 'friend in need and a friend indeed'. Exposure to the lack of soul in others when I am in distress can be one of the most harrowing experiences for me personally. We human beings should be supremely familiar with the spirit of comfort because it resides within us and only waits to be issued. Of all that is available to us of the creator god, the spirit of truth and comfort is at all times closest to us and most readily accessed by us, given that we recognize discomfort in someone else. All the same, we may need practice and application in this direction. Perhaps we tend to wallow in our discomfort? That is not the way to invite comfort. In fact that is a way to keep it at bay.

*

Now we need to review our reason for suffering pain. Let's think about what we are trying to achieve. What is our main reason for suffering? Are we mainly wanting to get rid of the pain or do we wish to accommodate the growth-change due to our blockage of which the pain exists in the first place? We need to make our mind up about that. Do we exist in accordance with a status quo that has been invented for us and we have all along obliged by supporting it or do we see ourselves as human beings who develop and then evolve, in other words who grow and are therefore interested in cooperating as much as possible and necessary with the various growth stimuli that engage our attention.

If the latter, then this essay is for us. If the former, we need to look elsewhere. From the christian Gospels, for example, we might learn about this growth-process in terms of resurrection, which is described there as the process whereby we rise out of the inert status quo and gradually recover our various inborn human-natural faculties with the help of the examples that have been set by the one who initially accomplished that evolutionary move and by those who in the meantime have also done so. During the last two-thousand years or so we have been influenced, whether we liked it of not, by those examples, especially by the initial one set personally for our benefit. So we can say that our very human nature is endowed from birth – not only with the potential for personal perfection but also with the impossibility to return to those ancient ways when human perfection was only still a hope and a desire.

So you might say that we have inherited a model of human growth which we can get to know, if we are willing to take the trouble. We are certainly persuaded from within to take that trouble, even to the point that we become most unhappy if renewal is on the cards for us but we are not playing those cards. This may be due to a combination of ignorance and arrogance. To some extent we may have adopted the humanist fallacy that would persuade us to assume that we are in total, egotistic charge of all our growth processes. Such a set of blinkers can be difficult enough to remove. If we want to make sense of pain intelligently suffered we need to discover within ourselves and within our community the spirit in accordance with which all that is becomes.

Now to some, the very mention of such a spirit is anathema and all one can do is let them get on with their existence, lest it should happen that they experience their depravity. I don't think depravity is too strong a word, because to be deprived of good spirit, or to deprive oneself of it, for that matter, is surely similar to cutting off one's head and expecting to be able to lead a normal life. So when I speak of suffering in Christ I take advantage of good spirit in my life rather than cutting myself off from it.

One can understand those who insist on their sovereignty because they have grown up in the company of those who take no responsibility for themselves and simply hand over all their troubles and pains to the government of the day, to the most up-to-date experts on every-thing or to some superstition that corrodes their sense of self. So they may be right in their rejection of anything or anyone that pretends to be able to 'live for them', to take their existence off their hands, as it were. We need to look very closely at the possible causes that might have brought about a perverse attitude towards human exis-tence and life. But this is only important insofar it should dissuade us from judging anyone instead of looking to our own attitudes and convictions. If we want a spirit to lead our life for us we are looking at something like the spirit of death, which will on occasion accommodate us, to our detriment, of course. Or if the very notion of spirit turns us off, we might be smart to look around a bit, to widen our horizon.

What I mean by the creative spirit urges me on to do myself as much good as possible. Certainly what I mean by god is not only merciful good spirit of love but also creative. The creation that goes on all around us, with which we can cooperate, which we can assist or hinder, this is the original source of my understanding of growth, natural growth, and then human-natural growth. The lat-ter is, of course, our own special province of interest be-cause we can know and understand ourselves from both within and without, while all other beings are accessible to us only from without. So for example I see good spirit as active in all religions, all philosophies, sciences and arts but more or less successfully, because we do manage to get in the way by insisting on our own private or pub-lic points of view. In a nutshell, the god of Abraham, Isaac and Jacob and thereafter of Jesus of Nazareth and of those who espouse his teachings and know his presence in their very being – is the one for me. I wouldn't mention that if I didn't think that many of those who have a one-sided or distorted approach to some particular religion would become even more hardened in their unfortunate ways if I didn't. The spirit of criticism – this reaction to creative spirit – exists among us, after all, not so that we should take up with it but rather so that we might come to our true senses.

*

Right. So if we want to cooperate in our growth, perhaps in our resurrection, there is plenty of opportunity for initiative. Don't ever think that by sidelining your ego you are giving up your responsibility for your actions and behaviour. On the contrary, not until you recognize the spirit of growth within you that carries the blueprint for who you are, for what you should amount to and what you might achieve, can you really take matters in hand and exercise your combined willpower and intellectual capacity in the way that gains you a sense of meaning and purpose, a degree of success and satisfaction.

If the way I speak of god puts you off, perhaps because the very concept has been spoiled for you by those for whom god is an idol, an ideal or one of many surreptitious brain-inventions of man, then do not let that in itself dissuade you from my philosophy, which is soundly based on practice.

*

Pain perceived as punishment:

The automatic reaction to pain can take a great variety of forms, and guilt is not unusual. What have I neglected, we ask, or where have I gone wrong? Those who discourage us from taking guilt upon ourselves do not necessarily do us a service. At least one may assume they are not on the side of those who would cause us pain. However we do know by now how we would, for good reason, like to go about accepting the responsibility for our reaction, especially since the only alternative seems to be our 'getting back' at something or someone. So is it possible that we might cope with any attachment of guilt as though it were simply meant for us, to remind us that we might be wise, not to say smart, to say: Yes of course, guilt, I understand. Not guilt that points out to us this or that misdemeanour, but merely an emotion suitable to the occasion – if we should choose now to suffer the pain? Is the guilt not simply an invitation to suffer? Can we distinguish the emotion from any cause we might be attaching to it? Whether guilt or shame, we may simply 'give in' to it, because the suffering is what counts, to relate us to our growth-process. Let us keep in mind, or recall to mind, if necessary, that we, as human beings, are defined as developing creatures, perhaps as evolving beings, so why should we resent any reminder at all of this if we are caught up in some awkward situation or implicated in some unpleasant procedure? The reminder is bound to be an emotion of some kind. This, as we know, is what emotions are for, to concentrate our attention on the way we are dealing or not dealing with what we would be smart to deal with.

Is all emotional guilt and shame of the nature of such a reminder? Very likely. Are all our pain-reactions coloured by emotion? Are they perhaps purely and simply emotions of one sort or another? Or let us instead ask:

15

What else could they be? In the absence of appropriate creative motion, there is emotion, and it is liable to hurt.

Of course we can deal creatively with emotions. We can use them as raw-material. Or we can simply give in to them and 'be as we were' – which would also be creative. Any kind of creativity which utilizes our emotions involves a kind of 'being as we were' too, this is worth mentioning. I am not describing two totally separate tactics here. It serves us well to be aware of both possibilities, both tactics, so that we may incline to one or the other if we so choose. They are tactics for dealing with negative feeling at the onset of pain – of death, if you like – not, I repeat, so that we will be rid of the pain but so that we will return to our growth-path, or to our peculiar-to-us resurrection process. As soon as we have returned there will be no pain.

All the while let us try as best we can to keep in mind that we are no mechanics. At best we are cooperating with the author of our created being. This creative authority knows better than we do what is good for us. We cannot make ourselves develop and evolve, no matter how many of our more or less culpable or shameful obstructions we succeed in removing. Nor do we ever know how far we have strayed – or not yet caught up. So we have to play it by ear too. Always and again we do not know that the race is over until we are past the finishing line. We never know how close we are to it during the race. There will be those who will know what I mean when I repeat the injunction: Always pray.

*

16

Pain of the soul:

Who does not know what it means only to wish for what we cannot have? To long for limitations and to be unwilling to set them for ourselves? We step into the river to bathe and when he current tugs at us we are afraid to raise our feet from the ground. This eternal fear of other destinations! The crowded streets, almost our movements are limited to a single step at a time while our spirit desires to flood the universe with joy, with gratitude. We have only heard of love, especially of the love that makes us forget the diseases, the acquired and cozening illnesses, where are their rewards? We see a young man perched upon the tip of a spire in the city and a tiny voice whispers: Why can this not be you? – even while we fully feel within our empty hearts the foolishness of such an act. Some toy with death because death is the closest thing to life they know.

How can our soul be in pain? Or painful, which is not the same? What is this procrustean bed we fabricate for our inwardness, for the free and luminous space, there to delight us? Who has spoiled for us the sheer delight of action for its own sake? Such an immensity of what is possible, constricted – cramped, left in a dark corner, cast aside as though of no value – for the lack of what? Whence the understanding that cures our soul?

Some have learned to sing the pain of their soul – the pain that is their soul. We hear them and learn to wonder. Now we chide ourselves for thinking too much or for thinking too little, for allowing ourselves to be upset by a flurry of excitement or by boredom. We may even throw ourselves into some activity as though we cared not for all the care in the world and then fatigue sets in which we stupidly view as a punishment. Whence this plurality of rewards and punishments? Our soul wants nothing to do with them. It seeks to disport itself, yes, innocently and never in a fever or to prove a point. If we were to learn how to listen to our souls true wishes we would know these wishes as our own and we would respect and honour them, not walk over them with careless feet.

Pain of the soul is not the soul but our soul, announcing itself to our jaded senses. Now is the time to listen carefully and lovingly to these cries of the soul which are really our own cries for help – for help which we must clearly understand before we can taste it, embellish it, assimilate it and offer it. Soul-pain is selfishness become characteristic. The psyche turns in its bed, now to the wall, now to the curtained window. It waits for a signal. Where should this signal originate? Phenomena have no intentions. Dreams lack all purpose. Is mankind such an impossible concept that we allow it to depress us?

A soul in pain – a misnomer. It is we ourselves who are in pain, if we but faced this and dealt with it. How can our soul be in pain? Our soul is nothing but merciful good spirit's extension into our live body. It is god's investment of himself in us in the hope that we will return it increased. – And besides, come to think of it, what a pleasure it is, what true pleasure, to say yes to our soul as that which we hold in trust! I suppose a degree of honourable recognition and mutual regard is required. If we but learned to know and appreciate god on behalf of ourselves, how many doors into life would not open! Does god really desire us? Has god a longing for the many creatures upon the earth, all of which must wait for us human beings to recognize them as companions and friends? I believe that this is almost an essential thought, for us to turn into some pleasurable entertainment from time to time. God without us, the playground of theologians – god within us as our active and at times belligerent soul.

Yes, this is worth a quick peek. I have never enjoyed the company of those who suppose themselves in the possession of a sentimental-sentimentalizing soul, of a holiness shackled to low desires like possessiveness and self-regard. What is it that rises within me then; quite genuinely, I hasten to add? It is the belligerence of the betrayed soul. Come to think of it, it is nothing more than myself saying: my soul is no such thing. Any soul, anyone's soul, is no such thing. Not that god thanks me for standing up for my soul, no not that at all, but simply I need to protect myself against such an often quite blatant falsehood and lie – a sickly, morbid, self-indulgent soul. I need to spit. It is piety taken to the extremes of the popular status quo. Happy the husband who has a wife with a soul capable of being bellicose! Should she not make war against his lazy, dreamy incontinence? If no one else does it, if circumstances cannot reach him, then thankfully his helpmeet speaks loudly and rudely against his culpable neglect. Let him know how to thank her for it – a little later, of course, when the pain has subsided.

Is it really any wonder that we feel an acute and soul-destroying pain when someone attacks our worm-eaten self? And on reflection, are we not glad that our worm-eaten self was destroyed? Of course it hurts. Whatever we are attached to, if it is forcibly removed, oh how that hurts! And again, this is no soul-pain; our soul does not hurt. What an imposition that someone should accuse us of having hurt his soul! All I have to do is behave fairly truthfully for voices to be raised against me. The situation is such, my friend, that due to your outlandish behaviour you 'got your come-uppance'. Now do the decent thing and suffer your pain, so that you may rejoin the community of those who are more honest with themselves and one another.

'Be kind,' we are told. 'Above all else, hurt no one's feelings. Let everyone stumble along and compliment them on their majestic gait. Steer a safe course. Do not project yourself into foreign troubles. Strive to be liked and accepted.'

But what of my soul, you say!

'What has your soul to do with it? Your soul is a husk left over from centuries of a dubious Christianity. The fashion today in the best circles is uiversal toleration. Best not to speak at all, because if you open your mouth, how can you avoid the sexist, racist, humanist remark? You cannot. Someone will pull you up for it and then all hell breaks loose. So lie low. Smile. Cherish the society of those who smile until their face turns into a non-belligerent mask.'

No, this is bad advice. I may not know anything about a soul but I know what it means to be honest and forthright. I also know how I feel when I have let myself down. No one has noticed, but what does that matter? Do I have a conscience? A social conscience? A Christian conscience? Not really. Not if you put it that way. I know the value of conscientious behaviour. If I have made a mistake I try to rectify it. If I have hurt someone, I apologize. But not everyone who insists I have hurt him or her is speaking the truth, so that is a question in itself. How did I hurt you? I can see that you hurt, but how am I responsible? Please explain. Is it not rather a case of you being unwilling to take the responsibility for your reaction? By trying to make me responsible you cheat yourself of a crucial ethical benefit.

Those who have grown into the habit of burdening their soul with foreign guilt need our help. It is such an unfortunate habit. I fear it may be a bad weakness. Let us not blame them for this weakness, for they will immediately agree with us and add on to their weakness. Neither should we perhaps sympathize with them too much, because water runs off a duck's back. Some call it tough love, what is required. But all love, if genuine, is tough; not feeble, not morbid, not simpering. Not overbearing, self-righteous, uncaring.

I feel here that god's humanity needs to be stressed. I explain god's humanity to myself – and of course to anyone willing to listen – as Christ. And what is Christ? It is definitely someone able to look after himself. Also, this Christ is capable of performances that astound me, largely because I cannot imitate them. The so-called *imitatio Christi* strikes me as a bit of a conundrum. God within us as human can be relied on, that's for sure, and I make a good habit of it, but I myself cannot take god's human tasks out of his hands. My soul has attributes both human and divine, for those are god's attributes since quite a long time now, so that I am justified in thinking of myself as both human and divine, but I am not both human and divine because of my own efforts and achievements, and this has to be kept in mind. I cannot and will not abide it, if that for which I am endlessly grateful is presented to me as though it originated in some individual who has placed the cart before the horse. Here he presents himself to me as god's gift to humanity. No, Christ is god's gift to humanity, let's keep that thought separate and clear. And it is those who follow or wait for Christ who are god's gift to humanity. If I want to take advantage of that gift, let me do it with the simplicity of a child and not pretend that I could just as well come up with the benefits myself.

As a matter of fact such a mistaken attitude may well be what has prevented you from coming up with a soul of your own. Reflect on that for a moment. A soul is a powerhouse, a dynamic potentiality, it is the motor of the car and it's up to you to start it but after that it, not you, delivers the momentum. In one way of putting it, Christ is more than willing to perform miracles for us but if we make all these efforts to perform them ourselves he stands back and waits. So you shout Gospel tracts and you promise to heal people and some of them may in fact mend but what about after that? Can you make that presumably healthy individual turn to god and turn into a personal human being with a head on his shoulders and a heart in its proper place? No you cannot. That, I am afraid, requires the sort of cooperative effort as when you know the difference between yourself and god.

So I say let us clear our road of mysticism. As soon as we become one with god, like the mystic, we are no longer human and that is a fault. Let us suffer for one another in Christ – but as rational or irrational human beings, aware of our divine humanity, without trying to upstage the central character of the play.

*

All else about us may change but our soul is that it is. All that we do and are in the absence of our soul is sooner or later bound to be painful. I say sooner of later because we are always at liberty to rely on our independent will and intellect and this makes it possible for us to drift into the backwaters where crocodiles still sleep or to scale the peaks of arrogance where we need to be rescued by helicopters. Emergencies take time to develop. In the meantime we think: Are we not enjoying ourselves, my goodness how smart we are, and we believe we have finally arrived. Well, it's true, we have arrived somewhere but hopefully the pain will set in sooner rather than later to alert us to our predicament.

Really there is no soul-pain, only psyche pain. Actually psyche is itself pain and if we grow up we learn to identify this pain correctly and to suffer it intelligently. Those who swear by their psyche seek to control it, to make it pay dividends, to lend a spurious veracity to their existence, so that they exist perpetually in pain which they service and manipulate and hide. Not until they come to the end of their tether is there any chance for them to listen to reason and sense. After all, we can try to base our entire existence on psychic phenomena, and this is a serious trial alright, and not only for us but perhaps even more for those around us. The best they can do is suffer us gladly. Maybe when we notice this we will catch ourselves on.

How readily we can come to grief since the modern industry is built around psychic survival. Many industries exist for no other reason than to safeguard our perpetual psychic enslavement. What with the arrival of the personal truth, it was unavoidable that opportunities for psychic diversions should become available. We cannot have true freedom unless at the same time we are at liberty to come up with soul substitutes. Why do we often even choose to come up with them? Because the truth that would set us free cannot help but point out to us at the same time the extent to which we have avoided it. So we cling to a psychic, bogus perfection in the forlorn hope of not being found out. As soon as we turn to merciful good spirit of love, our fears of being found out disappear and we become conscious of our capacity for soul-being. This consciousness however is not the end of the line. Soul-consciousness in itself is capacity and potential. Any attempt we make to stay put here is a recipe for decay. This, however, can be suffered too and when we notice it we do well to say to ourselves: The spirit that would entrust itself to me in terms of soul, must first have an outlet to others. We need to be, to behave and act, in terms of it and on the basis of it. We need to develop our own ways of showing how good spirit moves us. Our soul-works, as will soon become evident to us and others, are really quite different from psychic work. There is a definite trend in the direction of ourselves becoming more anonymous and our god becoming more glorious. The pleasure that comes along with this is not like the pleasure for which we have self-consciously laboured.

*

Our psyche is the pain incurred due to avoidance of soul.

All that we do to avoid soul first occurs as psyche. In view of the soul-life, psyche is pain. Once our soul is well out of the way, all our efforts in terms of psyche are judged by us, again, in terms of success and failure, pleasure and pain, cause and effect and so on. Our psychic pleasure is a horror to the god who wishes us well. It rates equally with psychic pain as the pain that would alert us to the fact of our error and to the availability of our cure and wellbeing. Constricted in the psychic mayhem we may ask for the wellbeing that we have, all ready, available to us within.

All pain is real or imaginary, and psychic pain is imaginary. It would be quite wrong of us to say that someone imagines, or 'only imagines' psychic pain, because that which is imaginary is not imagined yet. And remember that psychic pain is, in fact, all that is psychic. (We should not speak of 'our' psyche, as though such an entity could exist.) To someone who is constricted in psychic pain we should really say: 'Try to imagine what it is that ails you. Do actually imagine it and do not allow yourself to be swayed by a lot of images accidentally produced due to the fact that you are not in the possession of your soul.' This, of course, would place the emphasis on our ability to imagine, so that logically we would have to ask: Are we able properly to imagine in the absence of our soul?

The answer to this is: Yes, we are. Imagination arises from our human nature as cleanly and sweetly as any other human-natural product and all that is required of us, once we have left our dreamy childhood state behind us, is that we imagine distinctly and discretely; in other words, that we do nothing else while we imagine. So what else are we liable to do? We are liable to picture, or to try to picture, what we want to imagine. We are liable to accompany our imagination with wishful thinking. We are liable to imagine fearfully, in a constrained fashion, as though we were not allowed to imagine distinctly and needed someone's permission before we could imagine discretely. All this and more. Of course we cannot guard against such errors or set up boundaries and limits beyond which we dare not go in order to protect our distinct imagination. What we can do however is 'imagine like a child'. We cannot imagine like a child would, in our position; that is absurd, especially since children themselves still reside in their peculiar dreamy truth, which we cannot reproduce in ourselves. Childlike imagination however is a perfectly sensible concept and we do well to practice it and to have it on hand whenever we get into psychic trouble.

Imagination that rises from our human nature is therefore true. If that surprises you – in the light of what those say whose human nature is a psychic product and therefore 'sinful' or in some other way still in need of being 'saved', or freed, or reincarnated – take yourself to task and call to mind that someone has made it possible so that all human beings, if they choose, should be able to undergo a resurrection, the very initial impulse of which amounts to the revelation to us of our true human nature.

A lively, daily exercise of our distinct imagination therefore makes is much less likely that we are thrown off balance by psychic phenomena and also, which is equally important, the present availability, to us, of our imagination lets us quickly recognize psychic phenomena by their intrinsic falsehood. In the light of the fact that all that is modern is psychic or psychically determined, it would seem like plain and simple advice that we commence with our resurrection as soon as possible so as to minimize the pain in our life and to dispel once and for all the taste of death.

*

The very suggestion that we have within us a medium of truth and reality is probably anathema to most people. Some will say: Why should I be limited to some interpretation of the events that touch on my wellbeing and existence that is not entirely and wholly generated by myself? And when we look around and notice how readily 'the crowd' accepts whatever is dished up to it – or so it seems in any case – such an insistence on self-scrutiny is perfectly understandable. We want to be responsible for what happens to us and for what we instigate, whether painful or not, and we do not suppose that pain necessarily implies anything else except perhaps the cause of it.

However as soon as we speak of the cause of pain, the spirits divide. What it come down to in the end is how we view pain, especially at a time when presently we are not in pain or hurting. Do we see it, in itself, as fortunate or unfortunate. Certain wasting diseases, such a leprosy, would seem to encourage gratitude for our nerves as useful organs, so that when these organs register that something is amiss, we do not automatically shut them down and carry on as normal. At the same time, when we are depressed, we want to stop being depressed. Do we ask: Why am I depressed? the way we ask: Why does my leg hurt?

We know about pain of the flesh. Is there a pain of the spirit? 'Have you no spirit?' we ask someone who is listless and irresponsive. What do we have in mind? What sort of spirit do we mean? Is it something that makes us feel especially alive? Does it give us – or is it – 'get up and go'?

What sort of spirits might be on the average punter's shopping list – let's look at it that way.

Here we get into the realm of 'discernment of spirits'. Traditionally those who say they know something about this distinguish between divine spirit and 'merely human' spirit. The distinction between human and popular spirit seems to me more to the point, especially nowadays, when we can no longer trust those dyed-in-the-wool spirituality-mongers who tie their god to a system of concepts that leaves nothing to the imagination. However as soon as we exclude imagination from our daily lives, we go to extremes.

The fact that imagination, as a human faculty – not as a merely human faculty – can be falsified does not argue against imagination itself as restored human nature in action. The real argument however begins when we say that all human nature nowadays is 'restored'. It is restored to its original state of being and resides within us from birth, so that no matter how far we have strayed from our nature by self-will or allowed ourselves to be misguided by those who are not aware of this, our ability to return to our restored nature can never be totally lost by us or removed from us. The fact that we have Jesus of Nazareth to thank for this is of secondary importance. Of primary importance for any thinking human being must be his awareness of his sound human nature, as specifically demonstrated by his distinct imagination.

This is the imagination we see most distinctly exemplified by little children.

Now let us consider the following. What exactly is our restored human nature when we experience? Some would say this is not possible. Can we literally make contact with our human nature or is this an empty concept devoid of meaning except as a structural element for a pseudo-philosophical system or as some datum of a fashionable mind-game?

No, we experience our human nature, our restored human nature, as soon as we accept pain, any given moment of pain, as an increment of our creative mortality.

That pain should be linked with creativity is certainly not news to those of us who create on the basis of elemental impulses and in line with world-revelation. These may be the sources of our creative works whether we realize or not. However that the fact that we are liable to die, honestly and honourably accepted, should stimulate our living-experience, our live being, in the direction of creative good works, this cannot really occur to us until we suffer pain imaginatively, which is to say as mortal beings whose nature is divine.

*

We are natural inasmuch as we are born but we are also natural in terms of our behaviour, what we do, the

29

way we act and how we undergo or suffer this and that. We eschew artificiality. So while we still walk around feeling sorry for ourselves because we are 'only natural', no wonder that pain and death follow on our heels, barking and biting. While we suppose we are 'only natural' we are bound to pin our hopes to some supernatural realm or else we hanker for ideas with their promise of ideality.

An imaginative acceptance of all pain and of death as our friend, that is what we are after, and not as something that is an unavoidable evil. And pain as our friend does not hurt but it helps to transport us to the next stage of our development and to the next level of our evolution. We do not live senselessly. We have life and we want more. That is perfectly understandable. And if Christ is accessible to us as our restored human nature in person, then that is a benefit not to be sneezed at.

'In the name of Christ', we say, and Jesus is quoted as saying: What you do in my name, ask in my name, and so on; so it makes perfect good sense for us to ask how he means that. It needs to be talked and thought about not for the benefit of those who know perfectly well what is going on but for those who are perplexed.

*

What does it mean to do something in someone's name? Do we have to know that person? I cannot imagine how we could do it otherwise. And what if that person is no longer on the earth in the flesh? Then we would have to be able to remember that person. How can we today remember Jesus of Nazareth? I reckon we have to rely on our restored human nature to inform us, because that is where Jesus has left his impress. That is how he had made his mark in real history for all time.

So what do we have to do to remember Jesus? Clear our mind of all pictures, of all prejudice, of all preoccupation with things and ask that question again. How shall I go about remembering Jesus? And suddenly the wall that is built up brick by brick by clock-time and calendar-time crumbles, vanishes – no longer exists. You have remembered. You may do so whenever you wish. 'Come to me,' said Jesus, and you have just done that. You have done it this time by means of memory. There are many other means, but most depend on your finally not being inhibited by your notion of the passage of time.

*

Suffering pain imaginatively – therefore in terms of our human nature – which is restored, not by you, mind, to its pristine state and condition – .

Consider that the very pain you experience at times stems from your rejection of your restored nature. You resist and reject and oppose and contradict and criticize it in so many ways! Now why do you do that? I wouldn't blame you for it. No one would. What, exactly, is the problem you have with your restored nature? Here it suggests itself to you once again and you tighten up as if someone were about to knife you. Have you become so addicted to the crowd-mentality, to your individualism, to the massive state of the world, to the misconception that all is one and you are left outside in the cold and you peer through the curtained window into a cosy room, a homely fire burning, the family seated, to dinner or to prayer and when you knock they come shrieking to the

31

door to barricade you out because really they are a selfish bunch of fakers who can tell that you are in training for world without end? Be patient! Bear with the one who has made it possible for you to bear this pain and also to suffer it, so that you might etc. etc.

We are not to step outside our brief. We readily combine apparent oddities so that their true relation may shine forth.

*

So what we are suffering – when we do suffer intelligently and imaginatively – is our own objection to the truth. We are like children then and we suffer the divine ordinance to come onto us.

So do we equate Christ with the achievement of Jesus? I mean is there anything wrong with having at our disposal both the historic Jesus and the physical Jesus? We even have the mythic Jesus from the Gospel of John – not to mention a score of apocryphal writings. We are well supplied. We have nothing to complain about on that score. So why, in our right mind, would we want to thresh straw? We have biographies of Beethoven and we have his works. 'Oh my goodness!' I hear them roaring, the threshers of straw, 'Now he is equating Jesus Christ and Beethoven! Blasphemy!' Ignore them. They know nothing of degree. When I play a Beethoven Sonata on the piano I am in touch with Beethoven – and through him with Bach and through Bach eventually with Jesus. This is one line of spiritual progeniture. So what was in the beginning? For the creative scribe: the word. 'The word became flesh and made his dwelling among us.' Some nowadays don't like to use the word Christ at all.

Some are not aware of the Jesus within, the physical Jesus, who is mythically ours through his achievement, which is the restoration of our human nature. Others again use the name Jesus and the word Christ as though it were a magical shibboleth or totem. Finally we have to ask what it is that works for ourselves and maybe celebrate it, like I do, and then we leave everyone to deal with his or her obstinacy in his or her own way.

*

'Suffering in Christ' is after all intended here as a formula and as a memory aid, for the purpose of summing up a lively complex of thought and experience as I present it in this little essay. If it is our aim to obey merciful good spirit by thought, behaviour and action, then any suffering of death and pain we do will be, in reality, a suffering of the effects of our obstinacy, which effects will appear as caused from inside or outside us. What we have from within and from without, however, under normal circumstances, is spiritual justice, mercy and comfort, so we can see how what I have summed up as our obstinacy obstructs our access to these. Now whether our obstinacy was accidental or intentional, and since it makes no sense trying to distinguish which it was, it would seem most reasonable that we suffer in patient repentance and with an eye to the fact that god is on our side.

But why think of it as suffering 'in Christ'?

This is after all an experimental essay, so that we begin with a true insight which leads to cooperative experience.

Ignorance of the achievement of Jesus as the Christ, as the first to step into the spiritual reality in which human beings can finally evolve, may not be a major disadvantage for some, however to be aware of it as the major advantage that it is for those of us who are to aid and abet that evolution and who meanwhile are to evolve themselves, this, I should think, should count as essential. What the word Christ in that case stands for is guarantee of true evolutionary progress on the basis of salvation as freedom from death within us. If we were not free, we could not evolve. If we are meant to evolve but do not, we are in one kind of trouble. If we are not meant to evolve but pretend that we are, or that we should evolve, then this causes us another kind of trouble. By keeping Christ in mind, by believing in the one who made human evolution possible and who personally set it in motion, we are in the best possible position for being reminded in good time of the next evolutionary move. Such 'evolutionary moves' arise within us and we join in, as it were, to the extent of our sufficient appraisal of them and, of course, to the degree of our initial awareness of them.

Something, so it seems, is therefore to be said for our conscious 'being in Christ' in comparison to our historical and experiential awareness of Jesus. I dare say when Paul of Tarsus coined the formula 'Jesus Christ', rather than, for example, Jesus the Christ, he had something like this in mind. That he was aware of the evolutionary meaning of 'Christ' resides in his notion of the dying and living again with Christ within us.

What we today need to take into account is twenty centuries of modern reaction to the cosmic preconditions set into motion by Jesus plus the universal anxiety that is unavoidably the critical sign of that reaction which was indicated by Jesus himself as the abomination of desolation. It must be a sobering thought to many who would like to verify the authenticity of any evolutionary move before they 'join in', that this anxiety is really the only sign that is ever available. Since modernity leans ever so drastically in the direction of hypocrisy, (of pretending that we can be good or that we are good) much, needless to say, is made of the omnipresence of this sign while next to nothing is made of that which it signifies.

*

Unless we are in Christ, we cannot suffer in Christ. Since it is then in Christ that we do our suffering, the transformational aspect of it is unavoidable, and the nature of the transformation is always bound to be a case of 'living in relation to the world' changing to a 'living in world'. We cannot, obviously understand what living in world means unless we have at least once weathered this transformation due to our suffering in Christ. The equivalence of world with kingdom of heaven makes sense at least with respect to the fact that the term 'kingdom of heaven' does not refer to a supernatural state, as long as we realize simultaneously that the understanding of earth, and of life on earth, is not the same for those who relate to the world as for those whose world is spiritually set aside for them, to give them all the security they need whenever they are exposed, for reasons of potential creativity, to the modern world.

Of course we can sensibly speak of the world as modern since the translation of Jesus and the subsequent availability of being and suffering in Christ in the face of the now unavoidable duality of primitive, raw experience. Modernity, being the ongoing reaction to this duality in a million and one different guises, is a presentation, to the one in Christ, of the modern world on which he draws for the materials which he then shapes creatively for the benefit of all others who care to choose contemporary community on earth as the venue for their existence.

This reminds us once again of how suffering, of necessity suffering while being in Christ, is an essential ingredient of our creative work process. All who have the truth within them and can therefore be truthful, do work of one sort or another to make world as essentially eternal more obvious, more present. If for a moment we seriously reflect on the drastic difference between modernity and contemporary reality, we are bound to come close to understanding how an appropriation of creative matter from the modern world will be painful and downright deadly if not suffered. The only alternative is a kind of obstinacy, which is, in turn, reactive and the source of all we mean by modern creativity (certainly not what goes for 'modern art' in the modern world).

So one has the choice to suffer or to react. Modern individuals automatically react. When we ourselves react we become to that extent modern.

*

True contemporary creation shapes contemporary works and the meaning of such works is human being in eternal world.

So creative suffering in Christ shapes, rather than forming or structuring. A discussion of creative shape in comparison to form and structure would seem to lie not entirely outside the limitations we have set ourselves in the present essay.

*

What is shapely is sometimes considered to be formless and devoid of structure. In a superficial sense this is quite correct. Form and structure, however, are generally conceived as modern concepts, each with its dualistic counterpoint, so that one discusses – and criticises – form in relation to content, more or less – idealistically and never completely – one with it, and one speaks of structure as tight or loose and separately ascertainable from whatever is seen to be structured. So-called post-modern architecture, for example, comes up with 'deconstructivism'; or deconstruction in the latest post-modern philosophy questions the modern duality, is at least aware of it, however the putative process of 'dismantling' cannot have anything to do with creative shaping, which is the only way out of the modern reaction.

*

What we have in mind here is work, creative work, the work we do when we decide to do good. We call the process of this work creative inasmuch as the essence of it is transubstantial. An organic overcoming is involved. During the process, modern becomes contemporary. Duality becomes unity. Form and structure become shape.

Needless to say this process cannot be described in modern terms. The flower does not know itself; it has a presentiment, a premonition, a foreboding of the fruit. The fruit knows itself and remembers the flower. The

37

flower develops, the fruit evolves. The process from flower to fruit is organically creative, is evolutionary.

The comparison is somewhat, not altogether apt. The development of a lily in the field is never perverse, I dare say, but we are at liberty to indulge in all sorts of perversions while the evolutionary stage, still or again, terrifies us, so we unfortunately avoid it and hope we might be able to develop forever – dualistically, or even monistically, lately.

*

So keeping in mind that we are concerned with ethically good work here, we literally rely on cooperation with merciful good spirit throughout, and our achievement, our creation or product, is shapely. It has shape and is shapely. It continues to reflect upon itself, this creative spirit with which we are involved, while we contribute our human-natural resources, from within. The shape of the product could then be described as subtle, as articulate, as masculine or feminine. So shape is not monistic but whole. Cooperation with good spirit is essential – and is workable while we suffer in Christ. What we suffer is all that which at present is modern and needs to be transubstantiated.

*

Suffering in Christ is a physical process, organic throughout. Christ moves. He leads and we follow. Being in Christ is not like being in a good mood but more like an ongoing therapy. 'Come to me and I will set you free' becomes 'stay with me and continue to gain, and regain, your freedom as you work'.

The notion of work and growth, for a human being in evolution, is paramount. One is no longer concerned with salvation, which is really a modern exercise, but with one's resurrection, from period to period, as one proceeds in the light of one's salvation, which salvation is taken for granted.

What, is there no rest from work? But work itself is restful. Our willingness to suffer supposed setbacks, apparent errors of judgment, the stresses and strains for which we are liable to blame ourselves – all these become meaningful in Christ, where we know that we cannot be separated from god, though at times it should feel like it.

One of the modern attitudes to god allows us to remove the divine from relation to ourselves by envisioning God as sovereign, grand, benign, serene and most high; that sort of thing; while in reality god is involved in all our being and doing. However reality needs to be understood. It makes as little sense to say that God needs us to further his aims as to suppose that we need God to further our own aims. Ultimate aims, however remote, however supernatural or utopian, never truly play into the equation once our resurrection has commenced and we have begun to evolve. Especially our human-natural imagination needs to remain free of final suppositions.

We do not have life until we evolve but then we learn how to live in relation; while any escape from relation means pain and death and is therefore, as it were, well suffered out of existence and into a work.

*

While we suffer in Christ we know Christ as the centre – as the centre which holds. We journey out and return to the centre, and since this centre's location is not predictable, we need to know how to follow Christ – or perhaps to tarry at the centre. We may stay with Christ – or when we have stepped out of relation we may return to Christ, however this is only a figurative way of using our language. Human-naturally our focus is not on Christ or on god but on our work, as we exercise our creative love – as we love one another and are kind and respectful to people.

*

Suffering in Christ predisposes us human-naturally to creativity. It is the unwillingness to suffer in the face of the results due to our misbehaviour that brings about one crisis after the other. We feel we ought to behave more strenuously, more productively, however creative spirit cannot be content with this, since it is creative spirit that seeks to match us to our whole reason for being and doing. An absentmindedness in this department causes us to become ignorant of the purpose of pain, of the meaning of death, in the first place. Of course we may look ahead to the time when death no longer stings – which still leaves our imagination free to contemplate death as the by-product of superior creation, when we make allowances for the weakness that signifies god's strength and the doubts that are to reveal the certainty of Christ within us.

We are not to go beyond the remit of our inborne creativity. The fact that our very human nature dispels, from birth, all that would counter its welfare during growth (namely development and evolution) is no sooner acknowledged than we sense the consequence in our sinews and the integrity of our bones. How cruel that we should be coerced to achieve materialist goals and to abide by mechanical guidelines! However that is the trend of modern civilization, where modern implies being of two minds plus the inherent anxiety that comes along with that.

While pain and death are rejected as in the end negative and bad, we are stuck in our modernist/post-modern enclave wherein we tire, despair and decay in time, after however many bursts of obstinate self-glorification.

* * *

February 2018

www.ingramcontent.com/pod-product-compliance
Lightning Source LLC
Chambersburg PA
CBHW070340290526
45791CB00003B/1413